On Anarchism by James Guillaume
Prism Key Press | www.prismkeypress.com

ISBN: 978-1463691493

On Anarchism
James Guillaume

James Guillaume was born in London in February 1844. He became interested in anarchism when he was a student in Zurich, and later as a printer in Neuchatel. He became one of the leading members of the Jura Federation of the First International. Having accepted anarchist beliefs, he associated himself with Bakunin, with whom he was expelled from the International at the Hague Congress in 1872. Later he was active in founding the Anarchist St.-Imier International. He played a decisive role in Kropotkin's conversion to anarchism, and worked with him at anarchist agitation in Switzerland during the later 1870s. Early in the 1880s, Guillaume withdrew from anarchist activity, to become active again twenty years later in the anarcho-syndicalist movement. The four-volume work he wrote during this later period, *L'International: Documents et Souvenirs*, is the most important source of information from the anarchist point of view relating to the First International. Guillaume also edited Bakunin's Collected Works published in French in 1907.

Michael Bakunin: A Biographical Sketch

MICHAEL ALEXANDROVICH BAKUNIN was born on May 18, 1814 on his family's estate in the little village of Premukhino, in the province of Tver. His father was a career diplomat who, as a young attache, had lived for years in Florence and Naples. Upon his return to Russia, he settled down on his paternal estate where, at the age of forty, he married an eighteen-year-old girl from the prominent Muraviev family. Given to liberal ideas, he was for a while platonically involved with one of the Decembrist' clubs. After Nicholas I became Tsar, however, Bakunin gave up politics and devoted himself to the care of his estate and the education of his children, five girls and five boys, the oldest of whom was Michael.

At fifteen, Michael entered the Artillery School in St. Petersburg where, three years later, he was commissioned a junior officer and sent to garrison in the provinces of Minsk and of Grodno, in Poland. He arrived in the latter post shortly after the Polish insurrection of 1832 had been crushed. The spectacle of Poland terrorized shocked the gently bred young officer and deepened his hatred of despotism. Two years later, he resigned from the army and went to Moscow, where he lived for the next six years, spending some summer vacations on the family estate.

In Moscow, Bakunin studied philosophy and began to read the French Encyclopedists. His enthusiasm for the philosophy of Fichte, shared with his friends Stankevich and Belinsky, led Bakunin to translate, in 1836, Fichte's *Vorlesungen über die Bestimmung des Gelehrten* (Lectures on the Vocation of the Scholar). From Fichte, Bakunin went on to immerse himself in the philosophy of Hegel, then the most influential thinker among German intellectuals. The young man wholeheartedly embraced Hegelianism, bedazzled by the famous maxim that "Everything that exists is rational" – even though it also served to justify the Prussian state. In 1839 he met Alexander Herzen and the latter's friend Nicholas Ogarev, who had returned from exile to Moscow; but their ideas and his were too divergent at the time for a meeting of minds.

In 1840, aged twenty-six, Bakunin went to St. Petersburg and thence to Germany, to study and prepare himself for a professorship in philosophy or history at the University of Moscow. When, in the same year, Nicholas Stankevich died in Italy, Bakunin still believed in the immortality of the soul (letter to Herzen, October 23, 1840). In the course of his intellectual evolution, however, he came to interpret the philosophy of Hegel as a revolutionary theory. As Ludwig Feuerbach, in his *The Essence of Christianity,* arrived at atheism by means of Hegelian doctrine, so Michael Bakunin applied Hegel to bis own political and social ideas and arrived at social revolution.

From Berlin, Bakunin moved in 1842 to Dresden. There he collaborated with Arnold Ruge in publishing the *Deutsche Jahrbücher* ("German Yearbooks"), in which he first began to formulate his revolutionary ideas. His article "Reaction in Germany: A Fragment by a Frenchman" concluded with the famous declaration:

> Let us put our trust in the eternal spirit which destroys and annihilates only because it is the unfathomable and eternally creative source of all life. The desire for destruction is also a creative desire.

Herzen believed at first that the article had actually been written by a Frenchman, and wrote in his personal diary that "this is a powerful and firm appeal, a victory for the democratic party. The article is from beginning to end bound to arouse wide interest."

The illustrious German poet Georg Herwegh visited

Bakunin in Dresden, and the two men formed a lasting friendship. A resident of Dresden who also became Bakunin's devoted friend was the musician Adolf Reichel.

Within a short time the Saxon government became overtly hostile toward Ruge and his collaborators, and Bakunin and Herwegh left Saxony for Switzerland. There Bakunin came into contact with the German communists grouped around Wilhelm Weitling. In Bern during the winter of 1843-44, a lifelong friendship developed with Adolf Vogt, who later became professor of medicine at the University of Bern. When the Russian government demanded that the Swiss authorities deport Bakunin to Russia, he left Bern in February 1844, stopping first in Brussels and then in Paris, where he remained until 1847.

In Paris Bakunin again met Herwegh, the latter's wife, Emma Siegmund, and Karl Marx, who had arrived there in 1843. Marx at first collaborated with Arnold Ruge, but he and Engels soon went their own way and began to formulate their own ideology. Bakunin saw much of Proudhon, with whom he held night-long discussions, and was also on friendly terms with George Sand. The years in Paris were the most fruitful for Bakunin's intellectual development – it was then that the basic outlines of the ideas underlying his revolutionary program began to take shape, though it was not until much later that he freed himself entirely of metaphysical idealism. Bakunin himself informs us, in a manuscript written in 1871, of his intellectual relations with Marx and Proudhon during this period. He recalls that:

As far as learning was concerned, Marx was, and still is, incomparably more advanced than I. I knew nothing at that time of political economy, I had not yet rid myself of my metaphysical aberrations, and my socialism was only instinctive. Although younger than I, he was already an atheist, a conscious materialist, and an informed socialist. It was precisely at this time that he was elaborating the foundations of his system as it stands today. We saw each other often. I greatly respected him for his learning and for his passionate devotion – though it was always mingled with vanity – to the cause of the proletariat. I eagerly sought his conversation, which was always instructive and witty when it was not inspired by petty hate, which alas! was only too often the case. There was never any frank intimacy between us – our temperaments did not permit it. He called me a sentimental idealist, and he was right, I called him vain, perfidious, and cunning, and I also was right.

Bakunin offers the following characterization of Engels in his book *Statism and Anarchy:*

In 1845 Marx was the leader of the German communists. While his devoted friend Engels was just as intelligent as he, he was not as erudite. Nevertheless, Engels was more practical, and no less adept at political calumny, lying, and intrigue. Together they founded a secret society of German communists or authoritarian socialists.

In a French manuscript of 1870, Bakunin evaluates Proudhon, comparing him to Marx:

As I told him a few months before his death, Proudhon, in spite of all his efforts to shake off the tradition of classical idealism, remained all his life an incorrigible idealist, immersed in the Bible, in Roman law and metaphysics. His great misfortune was that he had never studied the natural sciences or appropriated their method. He had the instincts of a genius and he glimpsed the right road, but hindered by his idealistic thinking patterns, he fell always into the old errors. Proudhon was a perpetual contradiction: a vigorous genius, a revolutionary thinker arguing against idealistic phantoms, and yet never able to surmount them himself.... Marx as a thinker is on the right path. He has established the principle that juridical evolution in history is not the cause but the effect of economic development, and this is a great and fruitful concept. Though he did not originate it – it was to a greater or lesser extent formulated before him by many others – to Marx belongs the credit for solidly establishing it as the basis for an economic system. On the other hand, Proudhon understood and felt liberty much better than he. Proudhon, when not obsessed with metaphysical doctrine, was a revolutionary by instinct; he adored Satan and proclaimed Anarchy. Quite possibly Marx could construct a still more rational system of liberty, but he lacks the instinct of liberty – he remains from head to foot an authoritarian.

On November 29 1847, at a banquet in Paris commemorating the Polish insurrection of 1830, Bakunin delivered a speech in which he severely denounced the Russian government. At the request of the Russian Ambassador, Kiselev, he was expelled from France. To counteract the widespread protests of those who sympathized with Bakunin, Kiselev circulated the rumor that he had been employed by the Russian government to pose as a revolutionary, but that he had gone too far. (This is related by Bakunin in a letter to Fanelli, May 29, 1867.) Bakunin then went to Brussels, where he again met Marx. Of Marx and his circle Bakunin wrote to his friend Herwegh:

11

The German workers, Bornstadt, Marx, Engels – especially Marx – poison the atmosphere. Vanity, malevolence, gossip, pretentiousness and boasting in theory and cowardice in practice. Dissertations about life, action, and feeling – and complete absence of life, action, and feeling – and complete absence of life. Disgusting flattery of the more advanced workers – and empty talk. According to them, Feuerbach is a "bourgeois," and the epithet BOURGEOIS! is shouted *ad nauseam* by people who are from head to foot more bourgeois than anyone in a provincial city – in short, foolishness and lies, lies and foolishness. In such an atmosphere no one can breathe freely. I stay away from them and I have openly declared that I will not go to their *Kommunistischer Handwerkerverein* [Communist Trade Union Society] and will have nothing to do with this organization.

The revolution of February 24, 1848, opened the doors of France once again to Bakunin. just as he was about to return to Paris, however, events in Vienna and Berlin caused him to change his plans, and he left for Germany in April. He was also then hoping to participate in the Polish insurrectionary movement. In Cologne, he again met Marx and Engels, who had begun publication of their *Neue Rheinische Zeitung.* It was at this time that the "Democratic Legion of Paris" organized an expedition to Germany to stage an insurrection in the Grand Duchy of Baden. The attempt was a disastrous failure. Marx and Engels violently attacked Bakunin's friend Herwegh, who together with other German exiles was one of the leaders of this ill-fated expedition. Bakunin came to his defense. Much laterin 1871 – Bakunin wrote that "I must openly admit that in this controversy Marx and Engels were in the right. With characteristic insolence, they attacked Herwegh personally when he was not there to defend himself. In a face-to-face confrontation with them, I heatedly defended Herwegh, and our mutual dislike began then."

Later, in June 1848, Bakunin went to Berlin and Breslau and then to Prague, where he tried to influence the Slav Congress in a revolutionary democratic direction. After participating in the week-long insurrection, which was brutally suppressed, he returned to Breslau. He was still there when the *Neue Rheinische Zeitung* – controlled by Marx – published in its July 6 issue a letter from a Paris correspondent which read, in part:

> In regard to pro-Slav propaganda, we were told yesterday that George Sand possesses documents which greatly compromise the Russian exile Michael Bakunin and reveal him as an instrument or newly enrolled AGENT OF RUSSIA, who played a key part in the arrest of the unfortunate Poles. George Sand has shown these documents to some of her friends. [See *Neue Rheinische Zeitung* of 3rd August 1848]

Bakunin immediately protested this infamous slander in a letter published in the *Allgemeine Oder Zeitung* of Breslau, and reprinted in the *Neue Rheinische Zeitung* on July 16. He also wrote to George Sand asking for an explanation. She replied in an open letter to the editor of the *Neue Rheinische Zeitung:*

> The allegations of your correspondent are entirely false. There are no documents. I do not have the slightest proof of the insinuations that you make against M. Bakunin. I have never had, nor have I ever authorized any one else to cast, the slightest doubt on his personal integrity and devotion to his principles. I appeal to your sense of honor and to your conscience to print this letter immediately in your paper.

Marx printed her letter together with the comment: "We have fulfilled the obligation of the press to exercise strict vigilance over prominent public individuals and at the same time given M. Bakunin the opportunity to dispel suspicions which have been current in certain Paris circles."

It is useless to elaborate on the singular theory that it is the duty of the press to publish false and libelous accusations without attempting to verify the facts!

The next month Bakunin and Marx met again in Berlin, and a reluctant reconciliation was effected. Bakunin recalled the incident in 1871: "Mutual friends induced us to embrace, and during our conversation Marx remarked, half-smilingly, 'Do you know that I am now the chief of a secret communist society, so well disciplined that had I said to any member, "Kill Bakunin," you would be dead?" '

Expelled from Prussia and Saxony, Bakunin spent the rest of the year 1848 in the principality of Anhalt. There he published, in German, the pamphlet Appeal to the Slavs: By a *Russian* Patriot, Michael *Bakunin, Member* of the Slav Congress. In this work he proposed that revolutionary Slavs unite with the revolutionaries of other nations – Hungarians, Germans, Italians – to overthrow the three major autocracies of the time: the Russian Empire, the Austro-Hungarian Empire, and the Kingdom of Prussia; this would be followed by the free federation of the emancipated Slavic peoples. Marx criticized these ideas in the *Neue Rheinische Zeitung* of February 14, 1849:

> Bakunin is our friend, but this does not prevent us from criticizing his pamphlet. Apart from the Russians, the Poles, and perhaps the Turkish Slavs, no Slavic people has a future, for the simple reason that they lack the indispensable historical, geographical, political, and industrial conditions for independence and vitality.

14

Regarding the difference between Marx's and his own views on the Slavic question, Bakunin wrote, in 1871:

In 1848 we disagreed, and I must admit that his reasoning was more correct than mine. Carried away, enraptured by the atmosphere of the revolutionary movement, I was much more interested in the negative than in the positive aspect of the revolution. Nevertheless, there is one point on which Marx was wrong, and I was right. As a Slav, I wanted the emancipation of the Slavic race from the German yoke, and as a German patriot he did not admit then, nor will he admit now, the right of the Slavs to free themselves from German domination. He thought then, as he does now, that the mission of the Germans is to civilize – that is to say, Germanize – the Slavs, for better or for worse.

In January 1849 Bakunin secretly arrived in Leipzig. There, together with a group of young Czechs from Prague, he occupied himself with preparations for an uprising in Bohemia. In spite of the growing reaction in Germany and France, hope still lived, for there was more than one place in Europe where the revolution had not yet been crushed. Pope Pius IX, expelled from Rome, had been replaced by the Roman Republic, headed by the triumvirate of Mazzini, Saffi, and Armellini, with Garibaldi in command of the army. 'Venice, its freedom regained, heroically repulsed the siege of the Austrians; the Hungarians, rebelling against Austria under the leadership of Kossuth, proclaimed the defeat of the Habsburgs. And on May 3, 1849, a popular rebellion broke out in Dresden, provoked by the refusal of the King of Saxony to accept the constitution of the German Empire approved by the Frankfurt Parliament. The King fled, and a provisional government was proclaimed. For five days the rebels controlled the city. Bakunin, who had left Leipzig for Dresden in the middle of April, became one of the leaders of the rebellion and inspired the highest measure of heroism in the men defending the barricades against the Prussian troops. A gigantic figure of a man, already renowned as a revolutionary, Bakunin became the focus of all eyes. An aura of legend soon enveloped him. To him alone were attributed the fires set by the rebels; about him it was written that he was "the very soul of the Revolution," that he initiated widespread terrorism, that to stop the Prussians from shooting into the barricades he advised the defenders to take the art treasures from the museums and galleries and display them from the barricades – the stories were endless.

On May 9 the rebels – greatly outnumbered and outgunned – retreated to Freiberg. There Bakunin pleaded in vain with Stephen Born (organizer of the Arbeiter Verbruderung, the first organization of German workers) to take his remaining troops to Bohemia and spark a new uprising. Born refused, and disbanded his forces. Seeing that there was nothing more to be done, Bakunin, the composer Richard Wagner, and Heubner – a democrat, very loyal to Bakunin – went to Chemnitz. There, during the night, armed bourgeois arrested Heubner and Bakunin and turned them over to the Prussians. Wagner hid in his sister's house and escaped.

The role of Bakunin in this rebellion had been that of a determined fighter as well as a leading strategist. Even the hostile Marx felt obliged to acknowledge his outstanding contribution in one of his letters, some years later, to the New York *Daily Tribune* (October 2, 1852), entitled "Revolution and Counter-Revolution in Germany":

In Dresden, the battle in the streets went on for four days. The shopkeepers of Dresden, organized into "community guards," not only refused to fight, but many of them supported the troops against the insurrectionists. Almost all of the rebels were workers from the surrounding factories. In the Russian refugee Michael Bakunin they found a capable and cool-headed leader.

Conducted to the Königstein fortress, Bakunin spent many months in detention, and eventually was condemned to death, on January 14, 1850. In June his sentence was commuted to life imprisonment, and the prisoner was then extradited to Austria, at the request of the Austrian authorities. Bakunin was first jailed in Prague and then, in March 1851, transferred to Olmutz, where he was sentenced to hang. Once again his sentence was commuted to life imprisonment. He was brutally treated in the Austrian prisons: his hands and feet were chained, and in Olmutz he was chained to the prison wall.

Shortly thereafter, the Austrians handed Bakunin over to Russia, where he was imprisoned in the dreadful dungeons of the Fortress of Peter and Paul. At the beginning of his captivity, Count Orlov, an emissary of the Tsar, visited Bakunin and told him that the Tsar requested a written confession, hoping that the confession would place Bakunin spiritually as well as physically in the power of the Russian Bear. Since all his acts were known, he had no secrets to reveal, and so he decided to write to the Tsar:

> You want my confession; but you must know that a penitent sinner is not obliged to implicate or reveal the misdeeds of others. I have only the honor and the conscience that I have never betrayed anyone who has confided in me, and this is why I will not give you any names.

When the Tsar, Nicholas I, read Bakunin's letter, he remarked, "He is a good lad, full of spirit, but he is a dangerous man and we must never cease watching him."

With the outbreak of the Crimean War in 1854, the Fortress of Peter and Paul was exposed to bombardment by the English, and Bakunin was transferred to Schlusselberg prison. 'here he was attacked by scurvy, and all his teeth fell out. Let me now interject what I myself wrote the day after Bakunin died, stating only what he personally told me about the last period of his imprisonment:

> The atrocious prison diet had completely ruined his stomach (scurvy) so that anything he ate caused nausea and vomiting, and he could digest only finely chopped sour cabbage. But if his body was debilitated, his spirit was indomitable. It was this above all he feared, that prison life would break his spirit; that he would no longer hate injustice and feel in his heart the passion for rebellion that sustained him; that the day would come when he would pardon his tormentors and accept his fate. But he need not have feared: not for a single moment did his spirit waver, and he emerged from the purgatory of his confinement as he entered, undaunted and defiant....

> He recounted to us, also, that to distract his mind from his long, loathsome solitude, he found pleasure in mentally re-enacting the legend of Prometheus the Titan, benefactor of mankind. who while chained to the Caucasian Rock by order of Olympus, heard the sweet plaintive melody of the ocean nymphs bringing consolation and joy to the victim of Jupiter's vengeance.

It was hoped that with the death of Nicholas I Bakunin's situation would be to some extent alleviated. However, the new Tsar, Alexander II, personally crossed Bakunin's name off the amnesty list. Much later, Bakunin's mother went before the Tsar and begged him to have mercy on her son; but the autocrat answered, "Madame, while your son remains alive, he will not be freed." One day Alexander, while reading the letter that Bakunin had written his predecessor in 1851, remarked to his aide, Prince Goncharov. "But I don't see the least sign of repentance."

In 1857 Alexander was at last induced to relent, and Bakunin was released from prison and sentenced to perpetual exile in Siberia. He was given permission to reside in the Tomsk region. In the latter part of 1858 he married a young Polish girl, Antonia Kwiatkowski. Somewhat later – through the intervention of a relative on his mother's side, Nicholas Muraviev, Governor General of Eastern Siberia – Bakunin was permitted to move to Irkutsk. There he was at first employed by a government agency, the Amur Development Authority, and later in a mining enterprise.

Bakunin had expected to be freed quickly and allowed to return to Russia. But Muraviev, who was trying to help him, lost his post because he opposed the bureaucracy, and Bakunin realized that he could regain his liberty in only one way: escape. Leaving Irkutsk in mid-June 1861 on the pretext of business – alleged commercial negotiations and a government-authorized study – Bakunin arrived in Nikolaevsk in July. From there he sailed on the government vessel *Strelok* to Kastri, a southern port, where he managed to board the American merchant ship *Vickery,* which took him to Hakodate, japan. He went next to Yokohama, then in October to San Francisco, and in November to New York. On December 27, 1861, Bakunin arrived in London, where he was welcomed like a long-lost brother by Herzen and Ogarev.

I will briefly summarize Bakunin's activity during the six years after his return to Western Europe. He soon realized that despite his personal friendship with Herzen and Ogarev, he could not associate himself with the political line of their journal, *Kolokol* ("The Bell"). During the year 1862, Bakunin expounded his current ideas in two pamphlets: To My *Russian, Polish, and Other Slav Friends* and *Romanov, Pugachev, or Pestel?*

The outbreak of the Polish insurrection of 1863 found Bakunin trying to unite all men of action to render effective aid and deepen the revolution. But attempts to organize a Russian legion failed, and the expedition of Colonel Lapinski came to naught. Bakunin then went to Stockholm – where he was reunited with his wife – hoping to get help from Sweden. His plans all failed, however, and he returned to London. He next went to Italy, and in the middle of 1864 returned to Sweden. Thence he went back once more to London, where he again saw Marx, and then to Paris, where he was reunited with Proudhon. Finally he went back to Italy.

As a consequence of the war of 1859 and Garibaldi's heroic expedition of 186o, Italy then stood on the threshold of a new era. Bakunin remained there until 1867, living first in Florence and then in and around Naples. It was during this period that he conceived the plan of forming a secret organization of revolutionaries to carry on propaganda work and prepare for direct action at a suitable time. From 1864 onward he steadily recruited Italians, Frenchmen, Scandinavians, and Slavs into a secret society known as the International Brotherhood, also called the Alliance of Revolutionary Socialists. He and his friends also combated the devoutly religious followers of the republican Mazzini, whose watchword was "God 2nd Country." In Naples, Bakunin established the journal *Libertà e Giustizia* ("Liberty and justice"), in which he developed his revolutionary program.

In July 1866 he informed his friends Herzen and Ogarev about the secret society and its program, on which he had been concentrating all his efforts for two years. According to Bakunin, the society then had members in Sweden, Norway, Denmark, Belgium, England, France, Spain, and Italy, as well as Polish and Russian members.

In 1867 bourgeois democratic pacifists of many lands (though preponderantly French and German) founded The League for Peace and Freedom and convened a congress in Geneva which aroused wide interest. Although Bakunin had few illusions about the new organization, he hoped to propagandize its members in favor of revolutionary socialism. He attended the congress, addressed the delegates, and became a member of the Central Committee of the League. For a whole year he tried to induce the Committee to adopt a social revolutionary program. At the second congress of the League, in Bern in 1868, Bakunin and his colleagues in the Alliance of Revolutionary Socialists tried to persuade the congress to adopt unambiguously revolutionary resolutions. After several days of heated debate, however, the resolutions were voted down. The minority faction of revolutionary socialists then resigned from the League, on September 25, 1868, and that same day founded a – new, open – not secret – organization, called the International Alliance of Socialist Democracy. The Alliance's Declaration of Principles was written by Bakunin; a summary of his ideas, it was the product and culmination of the long period of ideological development he had begun in Germany in 1842. Among other things, it stated that:

> The alliance declares itself atheist; it seeks the complete and definitive abolition of classes and the political, economic, and social equality of both sexes. It wants the land and the instruments of labor (production), like all other property, to he converted into the collective property of the whole society for utilization by the workers; that is, by agricultural and industrial associations. It affirms that all the existing political and authoritarian States, which are to be reduced to simple administrative functions dealing with public utilities in their respective countries, must eventually be replaced by a worldwide union of free associations, agricultural and industrial.

The New Alliance affirmed its desire to become a branch of the International, whose statutes it accepted.

just a few weeks earlier (September 1) the first issue of a Russian-language journal, *Narodnoye Dyelo* ("Public Affairs"), had appeared, under the editorship of Bakunin and Nicholas Zhukovsky, and had published a "Program of Russian Socialist Democracy" – a program that coincided, in the main, with that of the Alliance. With the second issue, however, the editorship changed hands: the paper fell under the control of Nicholas Utin, who gave it an entirely different orientation."

The International Workingmen's Association was founded in London on September 23, 1864, but its structure and its constitution were not formally adopted until the first congress convened in Geneva, September 3-8, 1866. In October 1864 Bakunin again met Marx, whom he had not seen since 1848. Marx requested this meeting to re-establish friendly relations with Bakunin who had been estranged when, in 1853, Marx's *Neue Rheinische Zeitung* [*Neue Rheinische Zeitung* was closed down in 1849. – Editor] repeated the old libel that Bakunin was a Russian agent. Mazzini and Herzen defended Bakunin, who was at that time in a Russian prison. Later in 1853 Marx had declared in the English paper *Morning Advertiser* that he was Bakunin's friend and had personally assured Bakunin that this was still the case. At their reunion in 1864, Marx invited Bakunin to join the International, but Bakunin preferred to return to Italy to devote himself to his secret organization. Bakunin's decision was understandable. At that time the International, outside of the General Council in London and a few Mutualist workers from Paris, could hardly be considered an international organization, and no one could foresee the importance it later assumed. It was only after the second congress at Lausanne in September 1867, the two strikes in Paris, and the great strike at Geneva (1868) that it drew serious attention and its revolutionary capabilities could no longer be ignored. In its third congress, in Brussels in 1868, the theories of cooperativism and Proudhonist Mutualism were seriously challenged by those of revolution and collective ownership.

In July 1868 Bakunin became a member of the Geneva section of the International, and after resigning from the "League for Peace and Freedom" at its Bern Congress, he settled in Geneva in order to participate actively in the labor movement of the city. Intensive propaganda sparked the growth of the International. A trip to Spain by Fanelli (an Italian revolutionary socialist and coworker of Bakunin) resulted in the establishment of the International in Madrid and Barcelona. The French sections of French-speaking Switzerland united into a federation under the name "Romance Federation of the International" and in January 1869 launched their official organ, the magazine *L'Égalité L'Égalité* attacked the false socialists of the Swiss Jura (mountains) and won the enthusiastic support of a majority of the region's workers for revolutionary socialism. On various occasions, Bakunin came to the Jura to denounce what he called "collaboration between workers and employers, alliances – masked as cooperation – with bourgeois political parties and reactionary groups," gradually forming a lasting friendship with the militant workers. In Geneva itself, a conflict took place between construction workers, who were instinctively revolutionary, and the better-paid and highly skilled watch and jewellery workers, who called themselves "Fabrica" and who wanted to participate in election campaigns with the bourgeois radicals. Those of a revolutionary tendency had the powerful encouragement of Bakunin, who, in addition to his public addresses, formulated his program and exposed the opportunists in a series of notable articles such as "The Policy of the International" [see selection in present volume], printed in *L'Égalité*. As a result, the Bakuninists won out – although this victory proved, regrettably, temporary. Nonetheless, since the Belgian, Spanish, French, and French-Swiss sections of the International all favored collectivism, its adoption by a large majority at the next congress was assured.

The General Council of London refused to admit the

Alliance as a branch of the International because the Alliance would constitute what amounted to a second international body in the International, thereby causing confusion and disorganization. Unquestionably one of the motives for this decision was Marx's ill will toward Bakunin, whom the German regarded as a schemer aiming to "break up the International and convert it into his own tool." But in any case, irrespective of Marx's personal sentiments, Bakunin's idea of forming a dual organization was unfortunate. When this was explained to him by his Belgian and Swiss comrades, he recognized the justice of the General Council's decision. The Central Bureau of the Alliance, after consulting the members, dissolved the Alliance and the local group in Geneva became a simple section of the International which was then admitted to membership by the General Council in July 1869.

The fourth general congress of the International (Basel, September 6-12, 1869) almost unanimously endorsed the principle of, collective property, but it soon became evident that the delegates were divided into two distinct ideological groups. The Germans, Swiss-Germans, and English were state communists. The opposing group – Belgians, Swiss-French, French, and Spaniards – were antiauthoritarian communists, federalists, or anarchists who took the name "Collectivists!' Bakunin, naturally, belonged to this faction, which included the Belgian De Paepe and the Parisian Varlin.

The secret organization founded by Bakunin in 1864 was dissolved in January 1869 because of an internal crisis, but many of its members kept in touch with each other. The intimate circle attracted new friends, Swiss, Spaniards, and Frenchmen, Varlin among them. This free contact of men united for collective action in an informal revolutionary fraternity was continued in order to strengthen and give more cohesion to the great revolutionary movement which the International represented.

In the summer of 1869, Borkheim, a friend of Marx, repeated in the Berlin journal *Zukunft* ("The Future") the old libel that Bakunin was a Russian agent, and Wilhelm Liebknecht, a founder of the German Social Democratic party, at various times continued to spread this falsehood. When Bakunin met Liebknecht at the Basel Congress, he challenged him to prove his charges before an impartial "court of honor." Liebknecht explained that he had never personally slandered Bakunin, but had only repeated what he read in the papers, primarily the *Zukunft*. The court of honor unanimously found Liebknecht guilty and signed a statement to that effect. Liebknecht admitted that he was wrong and shook hands with Bakunin, who then set fire to the statement, using it to light his cigarette.

After the Basel Congress, Bakunin moved to Locarno, where he could live cheaply and where he would not be distracted while making a number of Russian translations for a St. Petersburg publisher (the first was of volume one of Marx's Das Kapital). Unfortunately, Bakunin's departure from Geneva left the field open for the political machinations of a group headed by the Russian immigrant Nicholas Utin. In a few months they disrupted the Russian section of the International, occupied the key posts, and seized control of its organ, *L'Égalité*. Marx entered into an alliance with Utin and his camarilla of pseudosocialists of the "Temple Unico," the old Masonic hall used as a meeting place for the Geneva International. Meanwhile, on March 28, Marx addressed his notorious "Confidential Communication" to his German friends in order to stir up hatred among the German Democratic Socialists against Bakunin. He represented him as an agent of the pan-Slavist party, from which, Marx declared, Bakunin received twenty-five thousand francs per year.

In April 1870, Utin and his Geneva conspirators engineered a split of the Romance Federation into two factions. The first faction, which took the name "Jura Federation," was in agreement with the Internationalists of France, Belgium, and Spain. They adopted a revolutionary antiauthoritarian position, declaring that "all participation of the working class in the politics of bourgeois governments can result only in the consolidation and perpetuation of the existing order." The other, the Temple Unico faction, backed by the London General Council as well as by the Germans and Swiss-Germans, believed in "electoral action and workers' candidates for political posts."

Bakunin was at that time preoccupied with Russian events. In the spring of 1869 he became friendly with the fiery young revolutionist Sergei Nechaev. Bakunin still believed at that time in the possibility of a vast peasant uprising in Russia, much like that of Stenka Razin. The second centennial of this great revolt of 1669 seemed almost like a prophetic coincidence. It was then that Bakunin wrote in Russian the manifesto Some Words to My Young *Brothers in* Russia and the pamphlet Science and *the Present Revolutionary* Cause. Nechaev soon returned to Russia, but was forced to flee again after the arrest of almost all his friends and the destruction of his organization. He reached Switzerland in January 1870. Nechaev then prevailed upon Bakunin to abandon the translation of Marx's Das Kapital which he had already begun, and to concentrate entirely upon Russian revolutionary propaganda. Nechaev also succeeded in obtaining money for his alleged "Russian Committee" from the remainder of the Bakhmetiev Fund for Russian revolutionary propaganda, which was administered by Ogarev.

Bakunin also wrote, in Russian, the pamphlet *To the Officers of the Russian Army*, and, in French, *The Bears of Bern and the Bear of St. Petersburg*. He edited a few issues of the new series of Kolokol and engaged in feverish activity for many months. In July 1870, when Bakunin realized that Nechaev was using him to attain a personal dictatorship by Jesuitical methods, he broke off all relations with the young revolutionist. He had been the victim of excessive trustfulness and of his admiration for Nechaev's savage energy. Bakunin wrote to Ogarev on August 21, 1870:

We have been pretty fine fools. How Herzen would have

laughed at us if he were still alive, and how right he would have been!! Well, all we can do is to swallow this bitter pill, which will make us more cautious in the future."

When the Franco-Prussian War of 870-7 broke out, Bakunin passionately followed the course of battle. To his friend Ogarev he wrote in a letter dated August 11, 1870, "You are only a Russian, but I am an Internationalist." To Bakunin, the crushing of France by feudal, militarist Germany would mean the triumph of the counterrevolution; and this defeat could only be avoided by calling upon the French people to rise en masse and throw out both the foreign invader and their own domestic tyrants who were holding them in economic and political bondage. To his socialist friends in Lyons, Bakunin wrote:

The patriotic movement is nothing in comparison with what you must now do if you want to save France. Therefore, arise my comrades to the strains of the *Marseillaise* which today is once again the true anthem of France palpitating with life, the song of liberty, the song of the people, the song of humanity. In acting patriotically we are (also) saving universal liberty. Ah! if I were young again, I would not he writing letters. I would be among you!

A correspondent of the *Volksstaat* (Wilhelm Liebknecht's paper) had reported that the Parisian workers were "indifferent toward the war." Bakunin felt that it was perverse to accuse the workers of an apathy which, if actually present, would be criminal on their part. He wrote to the workers that they could not remain indifferent to the German invasion, that they must absolutely defend their liberty against the armed gangs of Prussian militarism.

If France were invaded by an army of German, English,

Belgian, Spanish, or Italian proletarians, holding high the banner of revolutionary socialism and proclaiming to the world the final emancipation of labor, I would have been the first to cry to the workers of France: "Open your arms, embrace them, they are your brothers, and unite with them to sweep away the rotten remains of the bourgeois world!" ... But the invasion that today dishonors France is an aristocratic, monarchic, military invasion.... If they remain passive before this invasion, the French workers will betray not only their own liberty, they will also betray the cause of the workers of the world, the sacred cause of revolutionary socialism.

Bakunin's ideas about the situation facing French workers and the means that should be employed to save France and the cause of liberty were expressed by him in a small pamphlet which appeared anonymously, in September 1870, under the title *Letters to a Frenchman on the Present Crisis.*

Bakunin left Locarno on September 9, 1870, and arrived in Lyons on the fifteenth. On his arrival, a Committee for the Salvation of France, whose most active and determined member was Bakunin, was immediately organized to mount a revolutionary insurrection. The program of the movement was printed on a huge red poster and was signed by the delegates of Lyons, St.Étienne, Tarare, and Marseilles. Although Bakunin was a foreigner and his position therefore more precarious, he did not hesitate to add his signature to those of his friends, thus sharing their perils and their responsibilities. The poster proclamation first declares that "The administrative and governmental machinery of the State having become impotent is abolished," and that "The people of France [have] regained full control over their own affairs. ' . ." It then immediately proposes the formation in all the federated communes of Committees for the Salvation of France, and the immediate dispatch to Lyons of two delegates from each committee in the capital of each department of France, to form the Revolutionary Convention for the Salvation of France.

On September 28, a popular uprising put the revolutionists in possession of the Lyons City Hall; but the treason of General Cluseret, in helping to suppress an uprising he had endorsed, and the cowardice of some of those who had betrayed the trust of the people caused the defeat of the revolutionists. Bakunin, against whom the prosecutor of the Republic, Andrieux, had issued an order of arrest, fled to Marseilles where he remained in hiding for some time, trying to prepare a new uprising. In the meantime, the French authorities spread the rumor that Bakunin was a paid agent of Prussia and that the Government of National Defense could prove it. On its part, Liebknecht's Volksstaat, commenting on the twenty-eighth of September and the red poster proclamation, declared that "Not even the Berlin [government's] press could have better served Bismarck's plans."

On October 24, Bakunin, in despair over events in France, sailed from Marseilles on a ship returning to Locarno by way of Genoa and Milan. The day before his departure he had written the following to the Spanish Socialist Sentinon, who had come to France hoping to participate in the revolutionary movement:

> The French people are no longer revolutionary at all.... . Militarism and Bureaucracy, the arrogance of the nobility and the Protestant Jesuitry of the Prussians, in affectionate alliance with the knout of my dear sovereign and master, the Emperor of all the Russias, are going to command all Europe, God knows for how many years. Goodbye to all our dreams of impending Revolution!!

The uprising that broke out in Marseilles on October 31, only seven days after Bakunin's departure, confirmed his pessimistic prediction: the Revolutionary Commune which had been established when news of the capitulation of Bazaine reached Marseilles held out for only five days before surrendering to Alfonso Cent, who had been sent by Gambetta.

In Locarno, where he spent the winter in seclusion, battling against poverty and despair, Bakunin wrote the continuation of his Letters to a Frenchman, an analysis of the new situation in Europe. It was published in the spring of 1871 with the characteristic title, The Knouto-Germanic Empire and the Social Revolution. News of the Parisian insurrection of March 18, 1871 (the Paris Commune) lightened his pessimism. The Paris proletariat, at least, had lost neither their energy nor their spirit of revolt. But France, exhausted and defeated, could not be galvanized by the heroism of the people of Paris. The attempts in various provinces to spread the communalist movement (self-governing communes) failed, and the Parisian insurrectionists were finally crushed by their innumerable enemies. Bakunin, who had gone to stay with friends in the Jura to be nearer the French frontier, was unable to help and was compelled to return to Locarno.

But this time Bakunin did not give way to discouragement. The Commune of Paris, upon which all the reactionary forces concentrated their furious, venomous hatred, kindled a spark of hope in the hearts of all the exploited. The proletariat of the world saluted the heroic people whose blood ran in torrents for the emancipation of humanity. "The modern Satan, the great rebellion, suppressed, but not pacified!" exclaimed Bakunin. The Italian patriot Mazzini added his voice to those who cursed the Commune and the International. Bakunin wrote the Response *of* an Internationalist to Mazzini which appeared in August 1871 in both Italian and French. This work made a deep impression in Italy, and produced among the youth and the workers of Italy a climate of opinion which gave birth, toward the end of 1871, to many new sections of the International. A second pamphlet, The Political Theology *of* Mazzini and the

30

International, even further consolidated and extended the International. Bakunin, who by sending Fanelli to Spain had created the International there, was by his polemic with Mazzini also the creator of the International in Italy. Now he threw himself passionately into the struggle not only against the domination of the bourgeoisie over the proletariat, but against the men who were trying to install the principle of authority in the International Workingmen's Association.

The split in the Romance Federation (French-speaking Switzerland), which could have been healed if the London General Council had so desired and if the agents of that Council had been less perfidious, was aggravated to the point of irreversibility. In August 1870 Bakunin and three of his friends were expelled from the Geneva section because they had declared their sympathy for the Jura Federationists. Soon after the end of the Franco-Prussian War Marx's agents came to Geneva to revive the discords. The members of the now-dissolved Geneva section of the Alliance believed that they had given sufficient proof of their friendly intentions by dissolving their section. But the party of Marx and Utin did not cease its harassments: a new section, called "Propaganda and Revolutionary Socialist Action," formed by refugees from the Paris Commune and including old members of the Alliance section, was promptly refused admission to the International by the General Council. Instead of a general congress of the International, the General Council, controlled by Marx and his friend Engels, in September 1871 convened a secret conference in London, attended almost entirely by partisans of Marx. The conference adopted resolutions destroying the autonomy of the sections and federations of the International and giving the General Council powers that violated the fundamental statutes of the International and the conference. At the same time it tried to promote and organize, under the direction of the General Council, what it called "the political [parliamentary] action of the working class."

Immediate action was necessary. The International, a vast federation of groups organized to fight the economic exploitation of the capitalist system, was in imminent danger of being derailed by a little band of Marxist and Blanquist sectarians. The sections of the Jura; together with the "Propaganda and Revolutionary" section of Geneva, met in Sonvilier (November 12, 1871) and established the Jurassian Federation of the International. This association sent a circular to all the federations of the International urging them to jointly resist the usurpations of the General Council and to energetically reconquer their autonomy. The circular, among other things, declared:"

If there is an undeniable fact, attested to a thousand times by experience, it is the corrupting effect produced by authority on those who manipulate it. It is absolutely impossible for a man who wields power to remain a moral man....

The General Council could not escape this inevitable law. These men, accustomed to march at our head and to speak in our name, have been led by the very demands of their situation to desire that their particular program, their particular doctrine, should prevail in the International. Having become in their own eyes a sort of government, it was natural that their own particular ideas should appear to them as official theory, as they had the sole "freedom of the city" [unlimited power] in the Association whilst divergent views expressed by other groups appeared no longer the legitimate expression of opinions With rights equal to their own, but as veritable heresies....

We do not impugn the intentions of the General Council. The persons who compose it found themselves the victims of an inevitable necessity. They wanted in good faith, and for the triumph of their particular doctrine, to introduce into the International the principle of authority.

Circumstances appeared to favor their doctrine, and it appears to us quite natural that this school, whose ideal is THE CONQUEST OF POLITICAL POWER BY THE WORKING CLASS, should have believed that the International was going to alter its original structure and transform itself into a hierarchical organization directed and governed by the General Council....

But while we understand these tendencies we feel obliged to fight them in the name of that Social Revolution whose program is "Emancipation of the workers by the workers themselves." ...

The future society must be nothing else than the universalization of the organization that the International has formed for itself. We must therefore strive to make this organization as close as possible to our ideal. How could one expect an egalitarian society to emerge out of an authoritarian organization? It is impossible. The International, embryo of the future society, must from now on faithfully reflect our principles of federation and liberty, and must reject any principle tending toward authority and dictatorship.

Bakunin enthusiastically welcomed the Sonvilier circular and devoted 'all his energies to actively propagating its principles in the Italian sections of the International. Spain, Belgium, most of the French sections (secretly reorganized in spite of the Versailles reaction following the defeat of the Paris Commune), and most of the United States sections declared themselves in agreement with the Swiss-Jura Federation. It was soon certain that the attempts of Marx and his allies to capture the International would be repulsed. The first half of 1872 was marked by a "confidential circular" issued by the General Council, written by Karl Marx and printed as a pamphlet entitled *Les prétendues scissions dans l'Internationale* ("The Alleged Splits in the International").

Prominent Federalist militants and others seeking independence from the General Council were personally slandered, and the widespread protests against certain acts of the General Council were depicted as sordid intrigues by members of the old International Alliance of the Social Democracy (the Alliance) who, directed by "the Pope of Locarno" (Bakunin), were working for the destruction of the International. Bakunin gave his reaction to this circular in a letter: "The sword of Damocles that hung over us so long has at last fallen over our heads. It is not really a sword, but the habitual weapon of Marx, a heap of filth."

Bakunin passed the summer and autumn of 1872 in Zurich, where on his initiative a Slavic section was founded, composed almost entirely of Serbian and Russian students, which joined the Jura Federation of the International. Since April Bakunin had been in contact with Russian emigre youths in Locarno who organized themselves into a secret action and propaganda group. The most militant member of this group was Armand Ross (Michael Sazhin). In intimate contact with Bakunin from the summer of 1870 to the spring of 1876, Ross was the principal intermediary between the great revolutionary agitator and Russian youth.

Bakunin's propaganda during this period was an inspiration to the young Russians in the following years. Bakunin's dictum that the youth must "GO TO THE PEOPLE" had become an axiom within the populist movement. In Zurich, Ross established a Russian-language printing plant which in 1873 published *Istoricheskoye Razvitiye* Internatsionala ("ne Historical Development of the International"), a collection of articles translated from Swiss and Belgian socialist papers, with explanatory notes by different writers, and a chapter on the Alliance written by Bakunin. In 1874 Ross's press printed *Gosudarstvennost i Anarkhiya* ("Statism and Anarchy"). A conflict with Peter Lavrov and personal dissensions among some of its members led to the dissolution of the Zurich Slav section of the International in 1873.

in the meantime the General Council decided to convene a general congress for September 7, 1872. It chose to meet at The Hague for two main reasons: it was a location close to London, and thus allowed many delegates who agreed with Marx's policies or held fictitious credentials to get to the congress easily; at the same time, the location made it more difficult for delegates representing remote or legally 'banned federations to attend; there was no possibility, for example, of Bakunin's attending. The newly constituted Italian Federation refused to send delegates. The Spanish Federation sent four, the Jura Federation two, the Belgian Federation seven, the Dutch Federation four, the English Federation five. These twenty-two delegates, the only ones truly representing constituents of the International, made up the core of the minority. The majority of forty who, in reality, represented only themselves had already pledged themselves in advance to faithfully carry out the orders of the clique headed by Marx and Engels. The only decision of the congress with which we deal here is the expulsion of Bakunin [Guillaume was also expelled] from the International. This action was taken on the last day of the congress, September 7, after one-third of the delegates had already gone home, by a vote of twenty-seven for and seven against, with eight abstentions. A mock inquiry by a five-member commission, held behind closed doors, found Bakunin guilty of the charges made by the Marxist clique, and he was expelled on two grounds:

1. That a draft of principles and letters signed "Bakunin" proves that said citizen has tried to establish, and perhaps has succeeded in establishing, a society in Europe named "The Alliance' with rules on social and political matters entirely different from those of the International.

2. That Citizen Bakunin has made use of deceptive tricks in order to appropriate some portion of another person's fortune, which constitutes fraud; that further he or his agents resorted to threats lest he be compelled to meet his

obligations.

The second Marxist accusation refers to the three hundred rubles advanced to Bakunin for the translation of Marx's Das Kapital and the letter written by Nechaev to the publisher Poliakov.

A protest against this infamy, immediately published by a group of Russian immigrants, made these points:

> Geneva and Zurich, October 4, 1872. They have dared to accuse our friend Michael Bakunin of fraud and blackmail. We do not deem it necessary or opportune to discuss the alleged facts on which these strange accusations against our friend and compatriot are based. The facts are well known in all details and we will make it our duty to establish the truth as soon as possible. Now we are prevented from so doing by the unfortunate situation of another compatriot who is not our friend, but whose persecution at this very moment by the Russian government renders him sacred to us. Mr. Marx, whose cleverness we do not, like others, question, has this time at least shown very bad judgment. Honest hearts in all lands will doubtless beat with indignation and disgust at so shameful a conspiracy and so flagrant a violation of the most elementary principles of justice. As to Russia, we can assure Mr. Marx that all his maneuvers will inevitably end in failure. Bakunin is too well esteemed and known there for calumny to touch him. Signed: Nicholas Ogarev, Bartholomy Zaitsev, Vladimir Ozerov, Armand Ross, Vladimir Holstein, Zemphiri Ralli, Alexander Oelsnitz, Valerian Smirnov.

The day after the Hague Congress of September 5, 1872, another congress of the International – comprising delegations from the Italian, Spanish, Swiss-Jura federations, as well as representatives from American and French sections – convened in St.-Imier Switzerland. The congress stated that it unanimously:

Rejects absolutely all resolutions of the Hague Congress and does not recognize to any extent the powers of the new General Council named by it.

The Italian Federation had already affirmed, on August 4, 1872, the resolutions of the St.-Imier Congress, which the Jura Federation also adopted at a special meeting held the same day as that of the congress. Most of the French sections hastened to express their complete approval. The Spanish and Belgian federations endorsed the resolutions at their congresses held respectively in Cordoba and Brussels during Christmas week of 1872. The American Federation did likewise at its meeting in New York City on January 12, 1873. The English Federation, which included Marx's old friends Eccarius and Jung, refused to recognize the decisions of the Hague Congress and the new General Council.

On June 5, 1873, the General Council in New York, exercising the powers vested in it by the Hague Congress, suspended the Jura Federation, declaring it subversive. As a result, the Dutch Federation, which had been neutral, joined the other seven federations of the International, declaring on February 14, 1873, that it refused to recognize the "suspension" of the Jura Federation.

The publication by Marx and the little group that still remained faithful to him of a pamphlet filled with gross lies, entitled *The Alliance of the Social Democracy and the International* [written in French in the second half of 1873], only provoked the disgust of all those who read this product of blind hatred.

On September 1, 1873, the sixth congress of the International opened in Geneva. The Belgian, Dutch, Italian, French, English, and Swiss-Jura federations were represented and the Lasallean socialists of Berlin sent a telegram of greetings. The congress concerned itself with the revision of the statutes of the International, pronounced the dissolution of the General Council, and made the International a free federation without any directing authority over it:

> The federations and sections comprising the International each reclaims its complete autonomy, the right to organize itself as it sees fit, to administer its own affairs without any outside interference, and to determine the best and most efficient means for the emancipation of labor.

His lifelong battles had left Bakunin exhausted. Prison had aged him before his time, his health had seriously deteriorated, and he now craved repose and retirement. When he saw the International reorganized in a way that fulfilled the principle of free federation, he felt that the time had come to take leave of his comrades. On October 12, 1873, he addressed a letter to the members of the Jura Federation:

> I beg you to accept my resignation as a member of the Jura Federation and the International. I no longer feel that I have the strength needed for the struggle: I would be a hindrance in the camp of the Proletariat, not a help ... I retire then, dear comrades, full of gratitude to you and sympathy for your great cause – the cause of humanity. I will continue to follow, with brotherly anxiety, all your steps and I will greet with joy each of your new victories. Till death I will he yours. [For full text, see p. 351.]

He had but three years to live.

His friend, the Italian revolutionist Carlo Cafiero, invited him to stay in his villa near Locarno. There Bakunin lived until the middle of 1874, apparently absorbed by his new life, one in which he had at last found tranquillity, security, and relative well-being. But he still regarded himself as a soldier of the revolution. When his Italian friends launched an insurrectionary movement, Bakunin went to Bologna in July 1874 to participate. But the insurrection, poorly planned, collapsed and Bakunin returned in disguise to Switzerland.

At this time Bakunin and Cafiero became estranged. Cafiero, having sacrificed his entire fortune for the cause of the revolution, found himself ruined and was forced to sell the villa. Bakunin, unable to stay in Locarno, settled in Lugano where, thanks to his paternal inheritance sent to him by his brothers, he was able to support himself and his family. The temporary coolness between Bakunin and Cafiero did not last long, and friendly relations were soon re-established. But Bukunin's illness progressed, ravaging both spirit and body, so that by 1875 he was only a shadow of his former self. Hoping to find relief, Bakunin left Locarno for Bern to consult his old friend, Vogt, to whom he said, "I have come to be restored to health or to die." He was taken to a hospital, where he was affectionately attended by Dr. Vogt and another close friend, the musician Reichel.

In one of his last conversations, recalled by Reichel, Bakunin in speaking of Schopenhauer remarked:

All our philosophy starts from a false base; it begins always by considering man as an individual, and not as he should be considered – that is, as a being belonging to a collectivity; most of the philosophical (and mistaken) views stemming from this false premise either are led to the conception of a happiness in the clouds, or to a pessimism like that of Schopenhauer and Hartmann.

In another conversation, Reichel expressed his regret that Bakunin could never find time to write his memoirs. Bakunin replied:

And why should you want me to write them? It is not worth the effort. Today the people in all lands have lost the instinct of revolution. No, if I get a bit of strength back again, I would rather write an ethic based on the principles of collectivism, making no use of philosophical or religious phrases.

He died at noon on July 1, 1876.

On July 3, socialists from all parts of Switzerland arrived in Bern to pay their last respects to Michael Bakunin. At his graveside, eulogies were offered by some of his friends from the Jura Federation: Adhemar Schwitzguebel, James Guillaume, Elisee Reclus; by Nicholas Zhukovsky, representing the Russians; by Paul Brouse for the French Revolutionary Youth; by Betsien for the German proletariat. At a meeting after the funeral all were moved by one sentiment: to forget, upon the grave of Bakunin, all personal bickering, and to unite on the basis of liberty and mutual tolerance all the socialist factions in both camps. The following resolution received unanimous approval:

The workers gathered in Bern on the occasion of the death of Michael Bakunin belong to five different nations. Some are partisans of a Worker's State, while others advocate the free federation of groups of producers. But all feel that a reconciliation is not only very essential and very desirable, but also easy to establish on the basis of the principles of the International, as formulated in Article 3 of the revised statutes adopted at the Geneva Congress of 1873.

Therefore this assembly, meeting in Bern, calls upon all workers to forget the vain and unfortunate dissensions of the past and to unite on the basis of strict adherence to the principles enunciated in Article 3 of the above-mentioned statutes [autonomy of the sections].

Do you want to know how this moving appeal to forget past hatreds and to unite in liberty was answered? The Marxist Tagwacht of Zurich on July 8 printed the following:

Bakunin was regarded by many fair-minded men and good socialists as a Russian agent. This suspicion, doubtless erroneous, was aroused by the fact that Bakunin greatly harmed the revolutionary movement; it was the reaction which benefited most from his activity.

Similar malevolent accusations vented by the *Volksstaat* of Leipzig and the Russian-language *Vpered* of London compelled the friends of Bakunin to conclude that his enemies did not intend to desist from their campaign of hatred. Hence the Bulletin of the Jura Federation on September 10, 1876, faced with hostile manifestations, declared:

We desire, as our conduct has always established, the most complete reconciliation possible of all socialist groups: we are ready to extend our hand in friendship to all those who sincerely wish to struggle for the emancipation of labor. But we are at the same time determined not to allow anyone to insult our dead.

41

Will the time come when posterity will assess the personality and achievements of Bakunin with the impartiality that we have a right to expect? Further, can one hope that the wishes expressed by his friends on his freshly covered grave will someday he realized?

Ideas On Social Organization

The ideas outlined in the following pages can be effectively achieved only by means of a revolutionary movement. It takes more than a day for the great flood to break the dyke; the floodwaters mount slowly, imperceptibly. But once the crest of the flood is reached, the collapse is sudden, the dyke is washed away in the winking of an eye. We can distinguish, then, two successive acts, the second being the necessary consequence of the first. At first there is the slow transformation of ideas, of needs, of the motives for action germinating in the womb of society; the second begins when this transformation is sufficiently advanced to pass into action. Then there is a brusque and decisive turning point – the revolution – which is the culmination of a long process of evolution, the sudden manifestation of a change long prepared for and therefore. inevitable.

No serious-minded man would venture to predict exactly how the Revolution, the indispensable condition for social renovation, will come about. Revolution is a natural fact, and not the act of a few persons; it does not take place according to a preconceived plan but is produced by uncontrollable circumstances which no individual can command. We do not, therefore, intend to draw up a blueprint for the future revolutionary campaign; we leave this childish task to those who; believe in the possibility and the efficacy of achieving the emancipation of humanity through personal dictatorship. We will confine ourselves, on the contrary, to describing the kind of revolution most attractive to us and the ways it can be freed from past errors.

The character of the revolution must at first be negative, destructive. Instead of modifying certain institutions of the past, or adapting them to a new order, it will do away with them altogether. Therefore, the government will be uprooted, along

43

with the Church, the army, the courts, the schools, the banks, and all their subservient institutions. At the same time the Revolution has a positive goal, that the workers take possession of all capital and the tools of production. Let us explain what is meant by the phrase "taking possession."

Let us begin with the peasants and problems concerning the land. In many countries, particularly in France, the priests and the bourgeoisie try to frighten the peasants by telling them that the Revolution will take their land away from them. This is an outrageous lie concocted by the enemies of the *people*. *The* Revolution would take an exactly opposite course: it would take the land from the bourgeoisie, the nobles, and the priests and give it to the landless peasants. If a piece of land belongs to a peasant who cultivates it himself, the Revolution would not touch it. On the contrary, it would guarantee free possession and liquidate all debts arising from the land. This land which once enriched the treasury and was overburdened with taxes and weighed down by mortgages would, like the peasant, be eman~ cipated. No more taxes, no more mortgages; the land becomes free, just like the man!

As to the land owned by the bourgeoisie, the clergy, and the nobles – land hitherto cultivated by landless laborers for the benefit of their masters – the Revolution will return this stolen land to the rightful owners, the agricultural workers.

How will the Revolution take the land from the exploiters and give it to the peasants? Formerly, when the bourgeois made a political revolution, when they staged one of those movements which resulted only in a change of masters dominating the people, they usually printed decrees, proclaiming to the people the will of the new government. These decrees were posted in the communes and the courts, and the mayor, the gendarmes, and the prosecutors enforced them. The real people's revolution will not follow this model; it will not rule by decrees, it will not depend on the services of the police or the machinery of government. It is not with *decrees,* with words written on paper, that the

Revolution will emancipate the people but with *deeds*.

We will now consider how the peasants will go about deriving the greatest possible benefit from their means of production, the land. Immediately after the Revolution the peasants will be faced with a mixed situation. Those who are already small proprietors will keep their plots of land and continue to cultivate it with the help of their families. The others, and they are by far the most numerous, who rented the land from the big landowners or were simply agricultural wage laborers employed by the owners, will take collective possession of the vast tracts of land and work them in common.

Which of these two systems is best?

It is not a matter of what is theoretically desirable but of starting with the facts and seeing what can be immediately achieved. From this point of view, we say first that in this mixed economy the main purpose of the Revolution has been achieved: the land is now the property of those who cultivate it, and the peasants no longer work for the profit of an idle exploiter who lives by their sweat. This great victory gained, the rest is of secondary importance. The peasants can, if they wish, divide the land into individual parcels and give each family a share. Or else, and this would be much better, they can institute common ownership and cooperative cultivation of the land. Although secondary to the main point, i.e., the emancipation of the peasant, this question of how best to work the land and what form of possession is best also warrants careful consideration.

In a region which had been populated before the Revolution by peasants owning small farms, where the nature of the soil is not very suitable for extensive, large-scale cultivation, where agriculture has been conducted in the same way for ages, where machinery is unknown or rarely used – in such a region the peasants will naturally conserve the form of ownership to which they are accustomed. Each peasant will continue to cultivate the

45

land as he did in the past, with this single difference: his former hired hands, if he had any, will become his partners and share with him the products which their common labor extracts from the land.

It is possible that in a short time those peasants who remain small proprietors will find it advantageous to modify their traditional system of labor and production. If so, they will first associate to create a communal agency to sell or exchange their products; this first associated venture will encourage them to try others of a similar nature. They would then, in common, acquire various machines to facilitate their work; they would take turns to help each other perform certain laborious tasks which are better accomplished when they are done rapidly by a large team; and they would no doubt finally imitate their brothers, the industrial workers, and those working on big farms, and decide to pool their land and form an agricultural association. But even if they linger for sonic years ill the same old routine, even if a whole generation should elapse before the peasants ill some communes adopt the system of collective property, it would still not constitute a serious hindrance to the Revolution. The great achievements of the Revolution will not be affected; the Revolution will have abolished agricultural wage slavery and peonage and the agricultural proletariat will consist only of free workers living ill peace and plenty, even in the midst of the few remaining backward areas.

On the other hand, in large-scale agricultural operations, where a great number of workers are needed to farm vast areas, where coordination and cooperation are absolutely essential, collective labor will naturally lead to collective property. An agricultural collective may embrace an entire commune [autonomous regional unit] and, if economically necessary for efficiency and greater production, many communes.

In these vast communities of agricultural workers, the land will not be worked as it is today, by small peasant owners trying without success to raise many different crops on tiny parcels of unsuitable land. There will not be growing side by side oil one acre a little square of wheat, a little square of potatoes, another of grapes, another of fodder, another of fruit, etc. Each bit of land tends, by virtue of its physical properties, its location, its chemical composition, to be most suitable for the successful cultivation of certain specific crops. Wheat will not be planted on soil suitable for grapes, nor potatoes on soil that could best be used for pasture. The agricultural community, if it has only one type of soil, will confine itself to the cultivation of crops which can be produced ill quantity and quality with less labor, and the community will prefer to exchange its products for those it lacks instead of trying to grow them in small quantity and poor quality on unsuitable land.

The internal organization of these agricultural communities need not necessarily he identical; organizational forms and procedures will vary greatly according to the preferences of the associated workers. So long as they conform to the principles of justice and equality, the administration of the community, elected by all the members, could be entrusted either to an individual or to a commission of many members. It will even be possible to separate the different administrative functions, assigning each function to a special commission. The hours of labor will be fixed not by a general law applicable to an entire country, but by the decision of the community itself; but as the community contracts relations with all the other agricultural workers of the region, an agreement covering uniform working hours will probably be reached. Whatever items are produced by collective labor will belong to the community, and each member will receive remuneration for his labor either in the form of commodities (subsistence, supplies, clothing, etc.) or in currency. In some communities remuneration will be in proportion to hours worked; in others payment will be measured by both the hours of work and the kind of work performed; still other systems will be experimented with to see how they work out.

The problem of property having been resolved, and there

being no capitalists placing a tax on the labor of the masses, the question of types of distribution and remuneration become secondary. We should to the greatest possible extent institute and be guided by the principle *From each according to his ability, to each according to his need.* When, thanks to the progress of scientific industry and agriculture, production comes to outstrip consumption, and this will be attained some years after the Revolution, it will no longer be necessary to stingily dole out each worker's share of goods. Everyone will draw what he needs from the abundant social reserve of commodities, without fear of depletion; and the moral sentiment which will be more highly developed among free and equal workers will prevent, or greatly reduce, abuse and waste. In the meantime, each community will decide for itself during the transition period the method they deem best for the distribution of the products of associated labor.

We must distinguish different types of industrial workers, just as we distinguished different kinds of peasants. There are, first of all, those crafts in which the tools are simple, where the division of labor is almost nonexistent, and where the isolated worker could produce as much alone as he would by associated labor. These include, for example, tailors, shoemakers, barbers, upholsterers, and photographers. It must, however, be remarked that even in these trades, large-scale mass production can be applied to save time and labor. What we say, therefore, applies primarily to the transitional period.

Next in order are the trades requiring the collective labor of numerous workers using small hand-operated machinery and generally employed in workshops and foundries, printing plants, woodworking plants, brickworks, etc.

Finally, there is the third category of industries where the division of labor is much greater, where production is on a massive scale necessitating complicated and expensive machinery and the investment of considerable capital; for example, textile mills, steel mills, metallurgical plants, etc.

For workers operating within the first category of industry, collective work is not a necessity; and in many cases the tailor or the cobbler may prefer to work alone in his own small shop. It is quite natural that in every commune there will be one or perhaps several workers employed in each of these trades. Without, however, wishing to underestimate in any way the importance of individual independence, we think that wherever practical, collective labor is best; in a society of equals, emulation stimulates the worker to produce more and heightens morale; further, work in common permits each worker to learn from the experience and skill of the others and this redounds to the benefit of the unit as a whole.

As to the workers in the remaining two categories, it is evident that collective labor is imposed by the very nature of the work and, since the tools of labor are no longer simple individual tools but machines that must be tended by many workers, the machines must also be collectively owned.

Each workshop, each factory, will organize itself into an association of workers who will be free to administer production and organize their work as they think best, provided that the rights of each worker are safeguarded and the principles of equality and justice are observed. In the preceding chapter, while discussing the associations or communities of agricultural workers, we dealt with management, hours of labor, remuneration, and distribution of products. The same observations apply also to industrial labor, and it is therefore unnecessary to repeat them here. We have just said that particularly where an industry requires complicated machinery and collective labor, the ownership of the machinery of production should also be collective. But one point remains to be clarified. Will these tools belong to all the workers in each factory, or will they belong to the corporation comprising all the workers in each particular industry? [Corporation here is equivalent to industrial union.]

Our opinion is that the second of these alternatives is preferable. When, for example, on the day of the Revolution, the typographical workers of Rome take possession of all the print shops of Rome, they will call a general meeting and proclaim that all the printing plants in Rome are the property of the Roman printers. Since it will be entirely possible and necessary, they will go a step further and unite in a pact of solidarity with all the printing workers in every city of Italy. The result of this pact will be the organization of all the printing plants of Italy as the collective property of the typographical federation of Italy. In this way the Italian printers will be able to work in any city in their country and have full rights and full use of tools and facilities.

But when we say that ownership of the tools of production, including the factory itself, should revert to the corporation, we do not mean that the workers in the individual workshops will be ruled by any kind of industrial government having the power to do what it pleases with the tools of production. No, the workers in the various factories have not the slightest intention of handing over their hard-won control of the tools of production to a superior power calling itself the "corporation." What they will do is, under certain specified conditions, to guarantee reciprocal use of their tools of production and accord to their fellow workers in other factories the right to share their facilities, receiving in exchange the same right to share the facilities of the fellow workers with whom they have contracted the pact of solidarity.

The commune consists of all the workers living in the same locality. Disregarding very few exceptions, the typical commune can be defined as the local federation of groups of producers. This local federation or commune is organized to provide certain services which are not within the exclusive jurisdiction or capacity of any particular corporation [industrial union] but which concerns all of them, and which for this reason are called *public services.* The communal public services can be enumerated as follows:

A. Public works (housing and construction)

All houses are the property of the commune. The Revolution made, everyone continues for the time being to live in the same quarters occupied by him before the Revolution, except for families which had been forced to live in very dilapidated or overcrowded dwellings. Such families will be immediately relocated at the expense of the commune in vacant apartments formerly occupied or owned by the rich.

The construction of new houses containing healthy, spacious rooms replacing the miserable slums of the old ghettos will be one of the first needs of the new society. The commune will immediately begin this construction in a way that will not only furnish work for the corporations of masons, carpenters, ironworkers, tilers, roofers, etc., but will also provide useful work for the mass of people who, having no trade, lived in idleness before the revolution. They would be employed as laborers in the immense construction and road-building an d paving projects which will then be initiated everywhere, especially in the cities.

The new housing will be constructed at the expense of the commune, which means that in exchange for the work done by the various building corporations these corporations will receive from the commune vouchers enabling them to acquire all commodities necessary for the decent maintenance and well-being of their members. And since the new housing has been constructed at public expense, this system will enable and require free housing to be available for all.

Free housing might well cause serious disputes because people living in bad housing will compete with each other for the new accommodations. But we think that it would be a mistake to fear serious friction, and for the following reasons: First we must concede that the desire for new and better housing is a legitimate and just demand; and this just demand will stimulate the building workers to make even greater efforts to speed construction of good housing.

But while awaiting new construction people will have to be patient and do the best they can with the existing facilities. The commune will, as we have said, attend to the most pressing needs of the poorest families, relocating them in the vast palaces of the rich; and as to the rest of the people, we believe that revolutionary enthusiasm will stimulate and inspire them with the spirit of generosity and self-sacrifice, and that they will be glad to endure for a little longer the discomforts of poor housing; nor will they be inclined to quarrel with a neighbor who happens to have gotten a new apartment a little sooner. In a reasonably short time, thanks to the prodigious efforts of the building workers powerfully stimulated by the demand for new housing, there will be plenty of housing for all and everyone will be sure to find satisfactory accommodations.

All this may seem fantastic to those whose vision goes no further than the horizon of bourgeois society; these measures are, on the contrary, so simple and practical that it will be humanly impossible for things to go otherwise. Will the legions of masons and other building workers be permanently and incessantly occupied with the construction of new housing worthy of a civilized society? Will it take many years of incessant labor to supply everyone with good housing? No, it will take a short time. And when they will have finished the main work, will they then fold their arms and do nothing? No, they will continue to work at a slower pace, remodeling existing housing; and little by little the old somber quarters, the crooked filthy streets, the miserable houses and alleys that now infest our cities will disappear and be replaced by mansions where the workers can live like human beings.

B. Exchange

In the new society there will no longer be *communes in*

52

the sense that this word is understood today, as mere political-geographical entities. Every commune will establish a *Bank of Exchange* whose mechanics we will explain as clearly as possible.

The workers' association, as well as the individual producers (in the remaining privately owned portions of production), will deposit their unconsumed commodities in the facilities provided by the Bank of Exchange, the value of the commodities having been established in advance by a contractual agreement between the regional cooperative federations and the various communes, who will also furnish statistics to the Banks of Exchange. The Bank of Exchange will remit to the producers negotiable *vouchers* representing the value of their products; these vouchers will be accepted throughout the territory included in the federation of communes.

Goods of prime necessity, i.e., those essential to life and health, will be transported to the various communal markets which, pending new construction, will use the old stores and warehouses of the former merchants. Some of the markets will distribute foodstuffs, others clothes, others household goods, etc.

Goods destined for export will remain in the general warehouses until called for by the communes.

Among the commodities deposited in the facilities of the Bank of Exchange will be goods for consumption by the commune itself, such as food, lumber, clothes, etc., and goods to be exchanged for those produced by other communes.

At this point we anticipate an objection. We will probably be asked: "the Bank of Exchange in each commune will remit to the producers, by means of vouchers, the value of their products, before being sure that they are in demand; and if these products are not in demand, and pile up unused, what will be the position of the Bank of Exchange? Will it not risk losses, or even ruin, and in this kind of operation is there not always the risk that the vouchers will be overdrawn?"

We reply that each Bank of Exchange makes sure in advance that these products are in demand and, therefore, risks nothing by immediately issuing payment vouchers to the producers.

There will be, of course, certain categories of workers engaged in the construction or manufacture of immovable goods, goods which cannot be transported to the repositories of the Bank of Exchange, for example, buildings. In such cases the Bank of Exchange will serve as the intermediary; the workers will register the property with the Bank of Exchange. The value of the property will be agreed upon in advance. and the bank will deliver this value in exchange vouchers. The same procedure will be followed in dealing with the various workers employed by the administrative services of the communes; their work resulting not in manufactured products but in services rendered. These services will have to be priced in advance, and the Bank of Exchange will pay their value in vouchers.

The Bank of Exchange will not only receive products belonging to the workers of the commune; it will correspond with other communes and arrange to procure goods which the commune is obliged to get from outside sources, such as certain foodstuffs, fuels, manufactured products, etc. These outside products will be featured side by side with local goods. The consumers will pay for the commodities in the various markets with vouchers of different denominations, and all goods will be uniformly priced.

It is evident from our description that the operations of the Bank of Exchange do not differ essentially from the usual commercial procedures. These operations are in effect nothing but buying and selling; the bank buys from the producers and sells to the consumers. But we think that after a certain length of time the functions of the Banks of Exchange will be reduced without inconvenience and that a new system will gradually replace the old system: exchange in the traditional sense will give way to *distribution,* pure and simple. What do we mean by this?

As long as a product is in short supply it will to a certain extent have to be rationed. And the easiest way to do this would be to sell these scarce products at a price so high that only people who really need them would be willing to buy them. But when the prodigious growth of production, which will not fail to take place when work is rationally organized, produces an oversupply of this or that product, it will not be necessary to ration consumption. The practice of selling, which was adopted as a sort of deterrent to immoderate consumption, will be abolished; the communal banks will no longer sell commodities, they will distribute them in accordance with the needs of the consumers.

The replacement of exchange by distribution will first, and in a comparatively short time, be applied to articles of prime necessity, for the workers will concentrate all their efforts to produce these necessities in abundance. Other commodities, formerly scarce and today considered luxuries, will in a reasonable length of time be produced in great quantity and will no longer be rationed. On the other hand, rare and useless baubles, such as pearls, diamonds, certain precious metals, etc., will cease to have the value attributed to them by public opinion and will be used for research by scientific associations, as components of certain tools, e.g., industrial diamonds, or displayed as curios in museums of natural history.

C. Food Supply

The question of food supply is a sort of postscript to our discussion of exchange. What we said about the organization of the Bank of Exchange applies in general to all products, including foodstuffs. However, we think it useful to add in a special section a more detailed account of the measures dealing with distribution of the principal food products.

At present the bakeshops, meat stores, wine and liquor shops, imported food stores, etc., are all surrendered to private industry and to speculators and these, by all kinds of fraud, enrich themselves at the expense of the consumers. The new society must immediately try to correct this situation by placing under communal public service the distribution of all the most essential foodstuffs.

This must be borne in mind: we do not mean to imply that the commune will take possession of certain branches of *production*. No. Production in the true sense of the term will remain in the hands of the associations of producers. But, for example, what is involved in the production of bread? Nothing beyond the growing of wheat. The farmer sows and reaps the grain and transports it to the warehouses of the Bank of Exchange; his function as producer ends at this point. Grinding grain into flour or changing flour into bread is not production; it is work similar to that performed by various employees in the communal markets, work designed to put a food product, bread, at the disposal of the consumer. The same goes for meat, etc.

Thus viewed, it is only logical that the processing and distribution of foodstuffs – baking, slaughtering, winemaking, etc. – should be performed by the commune. Thus, wheat from the warehouses of the commune will be ground into flour in the communal flour mill (which will be shared with several communes); the flour will be transformed into bread in the communal bakeries and delivered to the consumers in the communal markets. It will be the same for meats: the animals will be slaughtered in the communal slaughterhouse and cut up in the communal butcher shops. Wines will be preserved in the communal wine cellars and bottled and distributed by special employees. Finally, all the other perishable food commodities will be kept fresh in communal warehouses and kept in glass enclosures in the communal markets.

Above all, immediate efforts must be made to institute the free distribution of certain essential foods, such as bread, meat, wine, dairy products, etc. When abundant food is available and free for all,, civilization in general will have taken a giant step forward.

D. Statistics

The main function of the Communal Statistical Commission will be to gather and classify all statistical information pertaining to the commune. The various corporations or associations of production will constantly keep up-to-date records of membership and changes in personnel so that it will be possible to know instantly the number of employees in the various branches of production.

The Bank of Exchange will provide the Statistical Commission with the most complete figures and all other relevant facts on the production and consumption of goods. By means of statistics gathered from all the communes in a region, it will be possible to scientifically balance production and consumption. In line with these statistics, it will also be possible to add more help in industries where production is insufficient and reduce the number of men where there is a surplus of production. Statistics will also make it easy to fit working hours to the productive needs of society. It win be equally possible to estimate, not perfectly, but enough for practical purposes, the relative value of the labor time involved in the various products, which will serve as the criteria for the prices of the Banks of Exchange.

But this is not all. The Statistical Commission will be able to perform some of the functions that are today exercised by the civil state, for example, recording births and deaths. We do not include marriage because in a free society, the voluntary union of a man and a woman will no longer be an official but a purely personal matter, not subject to, or requiring, public sanction.

There are many other uses for statistics: in relation to diseases, weather phenomena, in short, all facts which regularly gathered and classified can serve as a guide to the development of science and learning in general.

E. Hygiene

Under the general heading Hygiene, we have assembled the various public services which are indispensable to the maintenance of public health. First, of course, are medical services, which will be free of charge to all the inhabitants of the commune. The doctors will not be like capitalists, trying to extract the greatest possible profits from their unfortunate patients. They will be employed by the commune and expected to treat all who need their services. But medical treatment is only the curative side of the science of health care; it is not enough to treat the sick, it is also necessary to prevent disease. This is the true function of hygiene....

F. Security

This service embraces the necessary measures to guarantee to all inhabitants of the commune the security of their person and the protection of their homes, their possessions, etc., against deprivation and accident (fire, floods, etc.).

There will probably be very little brigandage and robbery in a society where each lives in full freedom to enjoy the fruits of his labor and where almost all his needs will be abundantly fulfilled. Material well-being, as well as the intellectual and moral progress which are the products of a truly humane education, available to all, will almost eliminate crimes due to perversion, brutality, and other infirmities. It will nevertheless still he necessary to take precautions for the security of persons. This service, which can be called (if the phrase has not too bad a connotation) the Communal Police, will not be entrusted, as it is today, to a special, official body; all able-bodied inhabitants will be called upon to take turns in the security measures instituted by the commune.

It will doubtless be asked how those committing murder and other violent crimes will be treated in the new equalization society. Obviously society cannot, on the pretext of *respect* for individual rights – and the negation of authority, permit a murderer to run loose, or wait for a friend of the victim to avenge him. The murderer will have to be deprived of his liberty and confined to a special house until he can without danger be returned to society. How is the criminal to be treated during his confinement? And according to what principles should his term be fixed? These are delicate questions on which opinions vary widely. We must learn from experience, but this much we already know: that thanks to the beneficent effects of education (see below) crimes will he rare. Criminals being an exception, they will be treated like the sick and the deranged; the problem of crime which today gives so many jobs to judges, jailers, and police will lose its social importance and become simply a chapter in medical history.

G. Education

The first point to be considered is the question of child support (food, clothes, toys, etc.). Today parents not only support their children but also supervise their education. This is a custom based on a false principle, a principle that regards the child as the personal property of the parents. The child belongs to no one, he belongs only to himself; and during the period when lie is unable to protect himself and is thereby exposed to exploitation, it is society that must protect him and guarantee his free development. It is also society that must support him and supervise his education. In supporting him and paying for his education, society is only making an advance "loan" which the child will repay when he becomes an adult producer.

It is society and not the parents who will be responsible for the upkeep of the child. This principle once established, we believe that we should abstain from specifying the exact manner in which this principle should be applied: to do otherwise would risk trying to achieve a Utopia. Therefore the application must be left to free experimentation and we must await the lessons of practical experience. We say only that vis-à-vis the child, society is represented by the commune, and that each commune will have to determine what would be best for the upbringing of the child; here they would have life in common, there they would leave children in care of the mother, at least up to a certain age, etc.

But this is only one aspect of the problem. The commune feeds, clothes, and lodges the children, but who will teach them, who will develop their best characteristics and train them as producers? According to what plan and principles will their education be conducted?

To these questions we reply: the education of children must be integrated; that is, it must at the same time develop both the physical and mental faculties and make the child into a whole man. This education must not be entrusted solely to a specialized caste of teachers; all those who know a science, an art, or a craft can and should be called upon to teach.

We must distinguish two stages in the education of children: the first stage, where the child of five or six is not yet old enough to study science, and where the emphasis is on the development of the physical faculties; and a second stage, where children twelve to sixteen years of age would be introduced to the various divisions of human knowledge while at the same time learning one or more crafts or trades through practice.

The first stage, as just mentioned, will be devoted to development of the physical faculties, to strengthening the body and exercising the senses. Today the powers of hearing, seeing, and manual dexterity are incompletely and haphazardly developed: a rational education, on the contrary, will by special systematic exercises develop these faculties to the highest possible degree. And as to hands, instead of making children only right-handed, attempts will be made to render children equally proficient in the use of the left hand.

And while the senses are developed and bodily vigor is enhanced by intelligent gymnastic exercises, the culture of the mind will begin, but in a spontaneous manner; the child win naturally and unconsciously absorb a store of scientific knowledge. Personal observation, practical experience, conversations between children, or with persons charged with teaching – these will be the only form of instruction children will receive during this first period.

No longer will there be schools, arbitrarily governed by a pedagogue, where the children wait impatiently for the moment of their deliverance when they can enjoy a little freedom outside.

In their gatherings the children will be entirely free. They will organize their own games, their talks, systematize their own work, arbitrate disputes, etc. They will then easily become accustomed to public life, to responsibility, to mutual trust and aid. The teacher whom they have themselves chosen to give them lessons will no longer be a detested tyrant but a friend to whom they will listen with pleasure.

During the second stage, the children, being ages twelve to sixteen, will successively study in a methodical manner the principal branches of human knowledge. They will not be taught by professional teachers but by lay teachers of this or that science, who are also part-time manual workers; and each branch of knowledge will be taught not by one but by many men, all from the commune, who have both the knowledge and the desire to teach. In addition, good books on the subject studied will be read together, and intelligent discussion will follow, thereby lessening the importance attached to the personality of the teacher.

While the child is developing his body and learning the sciences, he will begin apprenticeship as a producer. In the first stage of his education, the need to repair or modify toys will introduce the child to the use of simple tools. During the second stage, he will visit different factories and, stimulated by his liking for one or more trades, will soon finally choose the trade in which he will specialize. The apprentices will be taught by men who are themselves working in the factories, and this practical education will be supplemented by lessons dealing with theory.

In this way, by the time a young man reaches the age of sixteen or seventeen he will have been introduced to the range of human knowledge, learned a trade, and chosen the discipline he likes best. Thus he will be in a position to reimburse society for the expenses involved in his education, not in money but by useful work and respect for the rights of his fellow human beings.

In conclusion, we should make a few remarks on the relationship between the child and his family. There arc people who assert that the program of placing the child in the custody of society means "the destruction of the family." This doctrine is devoid of sense. As long as the concurrence of two individuals of different sexes is necessary for procreation, as long as there are fathers and mothers, the natural connection between the parents and the child can never be obliterated by social relations.

Only the character of this connection will be modified. In antiquity the father was the absolute master of the child. He had the power of life and death over him. In modern times paternal authority has been subject to certain restrictions. What, then, could be more natural, than that a free egalitarian society should obliterate what still remains of this authority and replace it with relations of simple affection?

We do not claim that the child should be treated as an adult, that all his caprices should be respected, that when his childish will stubbornly flouts the elementary rules of science and common sense we should avoid making him feel that he is wrong. We say, on the contrary, that the child must be trained and guided, but that the direction of his first years must not be exclusively exercised by his parents, who are all too often incompetent and who generally abuse their authority. The aim of education is to develop the latent capacities of the child to the fullest possible extent and enable him to take care of himself as quickly as possible. It is painfully evident that authoritarianism is incompatible with an enlightened system of education. If the relations of father to son are no longer those of master to slave but those of teacher to student, of an older to a much younger friend, do you think that the reciprocal affection of parents and children would thereby be impaired? On the contrary, when intimate relations of these sorts cease, do not the discords so characteristic of modern families begin? Is not the family disintegrating into bitter frictions largely because of the tyranny exercised by parents over their children?

No one can therefore justly claim that a free and regenerated society will destroy the family. In such a society the father, the mother, and the children will learn to love each other and to respect their mutual rights; at the same time their love will be enriched as it transcends the narrow limits of family affection, thereby achieving a wider and nobler love: the love of the great human family.

Social organization cannot be restricted to the local commune or the local federation of producers' groups. We will see how social organization is expanded and completed, on the one hand by the establishment of *regional corporative federations* comprising all the groups of workers in the same industry; and on the other by the establishment of a federation of communes.

We have already indicated in Section III what a corporative federation is. Such organizations in a rudimentary form exist in present society. All workers in a given trade or craft belong to the same organization, for example, the federation of typographical workers. But these organizations are a very crude sketch of what they will become in the new society. The corporative federations will unite all workers in the same industry; they will no longer unite to protect their wages and working conditions against the onslaughts of their employers, but primarily to guarantee the mutual use of the tools of production which are the property of each of these groups and which will by a reciprocal contract become the collective property of the whole corporative federation. In this way, the federation of groups will be able to exercise constant control over production, and regulate the rate of production to meet the fluctuating consumer needs of society.

The corporative federation will operate in a very simple fashion. On the morrow of the revolution, the producers' groups [local unions] belonging to the same industry will find it necessary to send delegates from city to city to exchange information and learn from each other's experience. These partial conferences will prepare the way for a general congress of the corporative federation to be held at some central point. This congress will formulate a federative contract which will be submitted for the correction and approval of all the groups of the corporative federation. A permanent bureau, elected by the congress and responsible to it, will serve as the intermediary link between the groups of the federation and between the federation and all the other corporative federations.

When all the branches [industries], including the agricultural organizations, have been organized in this manner, they will constitute a vast federative network spanning the whole country and embracing all the producers, and therefore all the consumers. The statistics of production, coordinated by the statistical bureaus of every corporative federation, will permit the determination in a rational manner of the hours of labor, the cost price of products and their exchange value, and the quantities in which these products should be produced to meet the needs of the consumers.

People impressed by the hollow declamations of the so-called democrats will perhaps demand that all these details should be settled by a direct vote of all the members of the corporative federations. And when we reply in the negative they will accuse us of despotism; they will protest against what they consider to be the *authority* of the bureaus, arguing that the bureaus should not be invested with the exclusive power to deal

64

with such grave problems and to make decisions of the greatest importance. Our answer will be that the tasks performed by the permanent bureaus do not involve the exercise of any authority whatsoever. They concern only the gathering and classification of information furnished by the producers' groups. Once this information is combined and *made public,* it will be used to help fix prices and costs, the hours of labor, etc.

Such operations involve simple mathematical calculations which can yield only one correct result, verifiable by all who have access to the figures. The permanent bureau is simply charged to ascertain and make the facts known to everyone. Even now, for example, the postal service performs a somewhat similar service to that which the bureaus of the corporative federations will render in the future; and we know of no person who complains that the post office abuses its authority because it collects, classifies, and delivers the mail without submitting every operation to universal suffrage.

Furthermore, the producers' groups forming the federation will intervene in the acts of the bureau in a far more effective and direct manner than simply by voting. For it is they who will furnish all the information and supply the statistics, which the bureau only coordinates. The bureau is merely the passive intermediary through which the groups communicate and publicly ascertain the results of their own activities. The vote is a device for settling questions which cannot be resolved by means of scientific data, problems which must be left to the arbitrary decision of numbers. But in questions susceptible to a precise scientific solution there is no need to vote. The truth cannot be decided by vote; it verifies and imposes itself by the mighty power of its own evidence.

But we have only dealt with one half of the extracommunal organization; the federative corporations will be paralleled by the establishment of the Federation of Communes.

The revolution cannot be confined to a single country: it is obliged under pain of annihilation to spread, if not to the whole world, at least to a considerable number of civilized countries. In fact, no country today can be self-sufficient; international links and transactions are necessary for production and cannot be cut off. If a revolutionary country is blockaded by neighboring states the Revolution, remaining isolated, would be doomed. just as we base ourselves on the hypothesis of the triumph of the Revolution in a given country, we must also assume that most other European countries will make their revolutions at the same time.

In countries where the proletariat has managed to free itself from the domination of the bourgeoisie, the newly initiated social organizations do not have to conform to a set pattern and may differ in many respects. To this day there are many disagreements between the socialists of the Germanic nations (Germany and England) and those of the Latin and Slavic countries (Italy, Spain, France, and Russia). Hence, it is probable that the social organization adopted by the German revolutionists, for example, will differ on some or many points from what is introduced by the Italian or French revolutionaries. But these differences are not important insofar as international relations are concerned; the fundamental principles of the Revolution (see Sections I and II above) being the same, friendly relations and solidarity will no doubt he established between the emancipated peoples of the various countries.

It goes without saying that artificial frontiers created by the present governments will be swept away by the Revolution. The communes will freely unite and organize themselves in accordance with their economic interests, their language affinities, and their geographic circumstances. And in certain countries like Italy and Spain, too vast for a single agglomeration of communes and divided by nature into many distinct regions, there will probably be established not one but many federations of communes. This will not be a rupture of unity, a return to the old fragmentation of petty, isolated, and warring political states.

These diverse federations of communes, while maintaining their identity, will not be isolated. United by their intertwining interests, they will conclude a pact of solidarity, and this voluntary unity founded on common aims and common needs, on a constant exchange of informal, friendly contacts, will be much more intimate and much stronger than the artificial political centralization imposed by violence and having no other motive than the exploitation of peoples for the profit of privileged classes.

www.ingramcontent.com/pod-product-compliance
Lightning Source LLC
Chambersburg PA
CBHW060216290526
45789CB00003B/1289